BASIC FASHION DESIGN

PATRICK JOHN IRELAND

Basic Fashion Design

B. T. Batsford Ltd London

© Patrick John Ireland 1972
First published 1972

Printed in Great Britain by
Flarepath Printers Ltd
St. Albans, Herts.
for the publishers B. T. Batsford Ltd
4 Fitzhardinge Street, London W1

7134 2711 6

CONTENTS

INTRODUCTION

Before making any particular design, there are various factors which must be taken into account, especially when the design is for a specific market. These include:

Market outlet and price

Age group

Figure type

Consideration must also be given to:

1 Silhouette, line, fashion details, general effect
2 Suitability of the design for the purpose and occasion
3 Fabric, colour, texture and maintenance
4 Designing for various markets and areas—haute couture and mass production model wholesale and Boutique
5 Specialising in sportswear, eveningwear, beachwear, etc.

The designer, as a source of inspiration, will exploit historical events, social revolutions, films, theatre, sports, etc. A variety of materials may also inspire the designer, especially the more unusual types of materials such as vinyl, p.v.c., plastic, metal, paper and various synthetic fabrics. It is an advantage to keep in touch with the latest developments in materials frequently advertised through the press and by manufacturers.

Naturally it is an advantage if a designer is able to draw. It would be helpful to make a study of figure drawing and anatomy. However, if this is difficult then the method illustrated (page 10) will help beginners to create and develop their ideas on paper.

Sketch book : All designers should keep a sketch book, collecting ideas and details to be used for reference. In addition, a folder of sample fabrics—particularly new materials of interest—will be found most valuable.

Colour : Working out colour schemes should make the designer aware that colour can create different effects and illusions of shape. Experiment with paint creating different colour schemes; also use your collection of fabrics for the development of colour combinations.

Trimmings : Trimmings such as belts, chains, metal motifs, braids, etc. may also be a source of inspiration.

Total look : A studied use of the combination of colour, texture, silhouette, line proportions, balance, rhythm and unity, the designer achieves the successful 'total look'. The overall effect will be further enhanced by a careful selection of fashion accessories.

Methods of designing

Creating new ideas for a collection, selecting fabrics, colour ranges, and trimmings such as buttons, belts, fringing, braids, etc.

Designers use different methods when developing ideas for a collection.

Sketches can be produced and ideas developed from them. These may then be produced as a toile made in white cotton fabric or in the fabric of which the garment will be made, depending on the cost of the fabric.

A designer may also achieve a design by working directly with the fabric on the dress stand or on a live model. This will be done by draping, cutting and pinning the pieces together. The garment will then be made.

Some designers prefer to work on the flat pattern, by adapting the basic block and developing a design in this way, or all methods may be combined.

Design Exercise

You will notice that throughout the book I have suggested exercises in different chapters. When practising you should consider the sub-headings suggested with care:

Design Exercise: Exercise set introducing style features and processes, etc.

Occasion: Occasion when the garment would be worn

Season: Season, temperature, general conditions

Fabric: Suitable fabric for design considering season, occasion, maintenance and durability

Market Outlets: Place for garment to be sold, type of customer, age group

Silhouette

Silhouette is the shape or outline of a fashion created by the designer. Different silhouettes are achieved with the skill of cutting and by the use of different materials, trimmings, padding and corsetry. Silhouettes are constantly changing according to new fashion trends. The silhouette is achieved with material, cut, darts and seam placing.

Illustrated on the following pages you can see only a few of the possibilities of changing the silhouette.

Hem lines

Length of sleeve or width

Shape of skirt

Bodices

Panels—seam placing

Cutting on the bias

Blousing

Pleats

Padding

Stiffening

Frills

In conclusion the following considerations must be taken into account:

Line : The lines of the design are those within the silhouette referred to as the cut.

Proportion : Is the relationship between each part of the garment and the whole shape.

Balance : Balance is achieved when a design satisfies the eye, and when the composition of the garment is balanced.

Rhythm : Rhythm in design results from lines and masses that act as accents because they are repeated in an orderly, predictable rhythmic pattern. The main purpose of rhythm in design is to lead the eye to the focal point of interest in the design.

Unity : Unity of design is the element of good taste. Unity is the combination of silhouette, proportions, fabric structure, trimmings, etc. A garment lacks unity when it has been designed without consideration for the design elements.

Design Drawing

Place transparent paper over your diagramatic figure shape and design over the figure, remembering to relate the proportions of the design to the figure. Take care in the placing of the darts belts, buttons and pockets, etc.

It is a good idea to keep your sketches lined up as illustrated. This will enable you to compare your ideas as your designs develop. (see pp. 10–14).

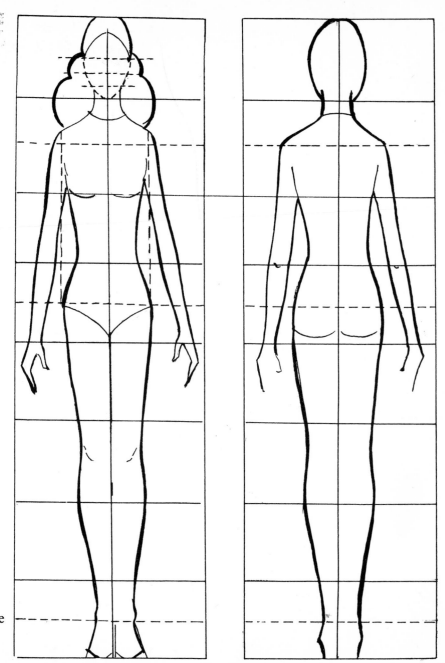

Sketch your basic figure shape
using the proportions
illustrated

Place layout paper over figure
shape and work out the design,
remembering to relate your
design to the proportions of the
figure

Complete design sketch, adding
details

Presentation sketch showing
back view, sample fabric, and
notes

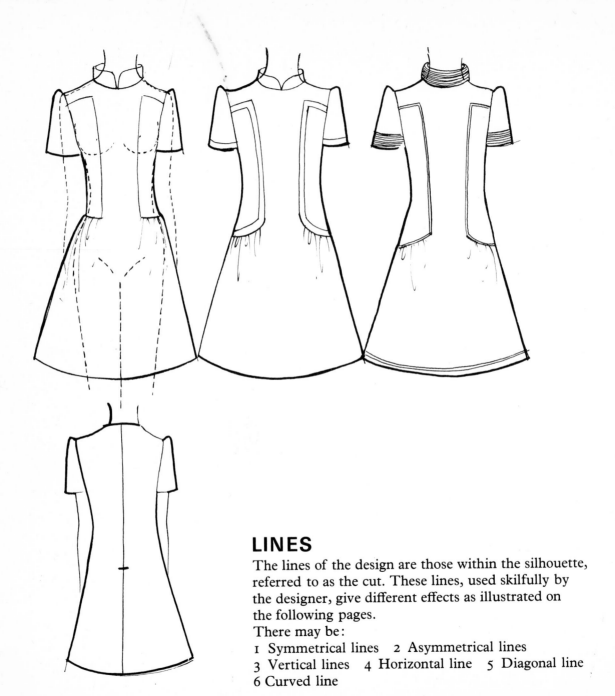

LINES

The lines of the design are those within the silhouette, referred to as the cut. These lines, used skilfully by the designer, give different effects as illustrated on the following pages.

There may be:

1 Symmetrical lines   2 Asymmetrical lines
3 Vertical lines   4 Horizontal line   5 Diagonal line
6 Curved line

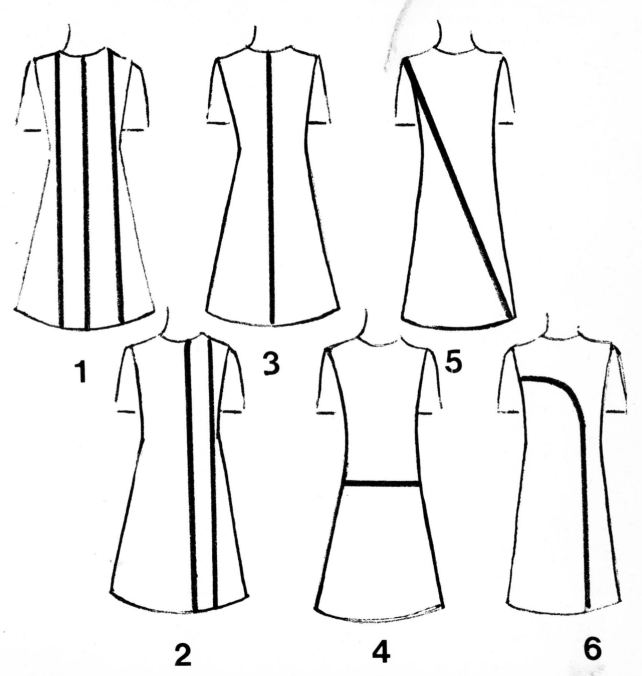

1   3   5

2   4   6

Symmetrical Balance is achieved when two masses of equal size and volume are placed at equal and opposite distances.

Asymmetrical Balance is achieved when the arrangement of the composition of line and detail is placed off balance.

1 Diagonal
2 Vertical
3 Horizontal

Diagonal and Vertical lines

Vertical and Horizontal lines

The Curve

Seams create lines. Listed are a few of the many seam treatments

Plain seam: The seam used to join two sections of fabric together

Plain seam top stitched: Used for decorative trimming as well as providing a strong seam

Slot seam: used as a decorative seam. A contrasting fabric, or fabric cut on the cross may be used

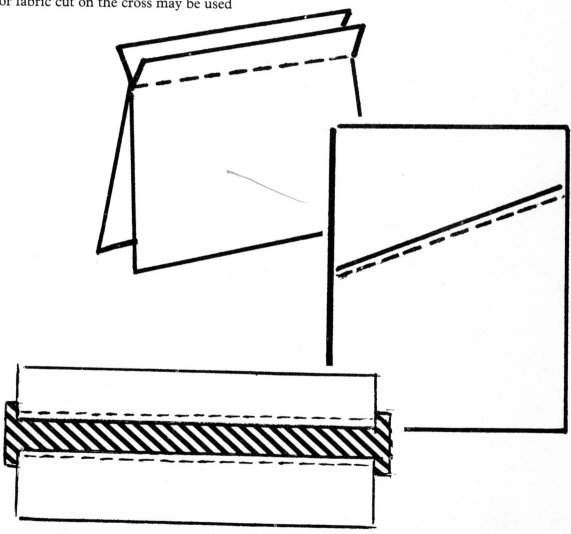

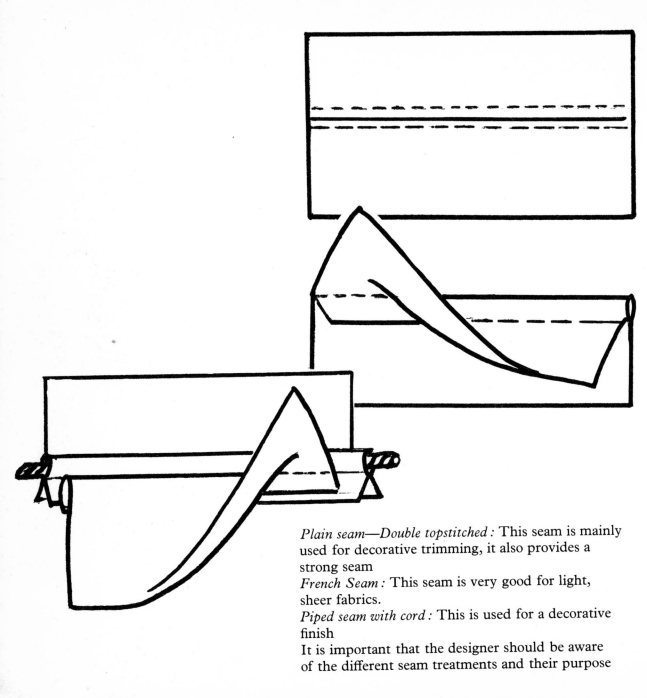

Plain seam—Double topstitched : This seam is mainly used for decorative trimming, it also provides a strong seam

French Seam : This seam is very good for light, sheer fabrics.

Piped seam with cord : This is used for a decorative finish

It is important that the designer should be aware of the different seam treatments and their purpose

Note the effects which can be achieved with the use of stripe material; lines may be used for figure flattery.

Use of line for figure flattery

Tall and slim : Soft curved and vertical lines avoid lines that would make the figure look too tall.
Short and slender : To make the figure appear taller, vertical lines and narrow front panels.
Short and round : Carefully controlled diagonal and vertical lines to make the figure look taller and slimmer.
Tall and heavy : Lines to make the figure slender without adding height. Diagonal lines.

Diagonal, Vertical, and Horizontal Lines

Design four dresses introducing diagonal, horizontal and vertical lines using contrasting materials, e.g. plain and patterned (as illustrated). You will be surprised how many variations you will create

Vertical and Diagonal Lines: Dresses designed in
contrasting materials using vertical and diagonal lines.
Note the selection illustrated above with interest in
yoke, bodice, waist and skirt emphasised by the use
of contrasting materials.

PROPORTIONS

Proportion is the relationship between each part of the garment and the whole shape. The relationship between bodice and skirt, size of pockets, collar, panels, belt, etc. (See illustrations)

An exercise in the relationship between the bodice
and the skirt. Note how one simple design can be
varied by the proportion of the bodice and skirt.

The bodice shape in relation
to the skirt

As an exercise design a day dress using the one design,
experimenting with the proportions of the design,
i.e. seam placing, collars, pockets, etc. in relation to
the silhouette. (See illustration)

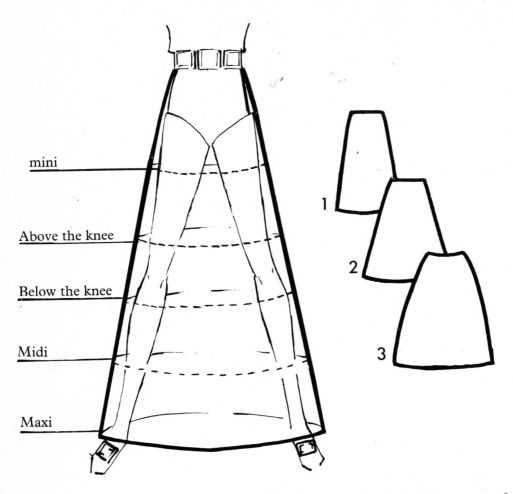

mini

Above the knee

Below the knee

Midi

Maxi

1

2

3

A skirt length is dictated by the current fashions, but the variations occur according to the occasion and trends.

The three basic skirt shapes:
1 Straight
2 Flared
3 Bell

Darts

Darts help to form the shape of the garment as well as being decorative. Illustrated are some examples of the placing of darts and the effects achieved. Note how all darts are centred towards the bust point. Darts usually end in a side seam, waist, shoulder or centre front seam and panel seams, as illustrated.

Fitting with seams and darts.
Seams may be used instead of
darts or they may be combined
for fitting

Design, as an exercise, one dress shape four times and
incorporate as many ways of fitting as possible,
introducing panel lines, darts, waist seams, folds,
tucks, gathers and unpressed pleats.

Day Dresses

Design a selection of day dresses introducing panel
lines as a feature incorporating the fitting in the seams
and panel lines.

Occasion : Summer holiday day dress
Season : Summer
Fabric : Printed linen
Colour : Own choice
Market Outlets : Medium price, Fashion store

The Yoke

The principle use of a yoke is to control fullness. In addition, the seam between the yoke and body of the garment may be a concealed dart.

Yokes also offer pure design-interest and may not have any fullness in connection with them at all.

Illustrated are only a few of the many variations of the yoke incorporated in a design.

Work out ideas and variations in your sketch pad, creating various shapes and introducing scallops pockets, etc.

Sports skirt

Design a selection of skirts suitable for country wear,
introducing yoke lines and pleats as a style feature.

Occasion : Casual wear suitable for the country
Season : Autumn
Fabric : Wool tweed
Colour : Colour of own choice
Market outlet : Medium price, Casual wear department
in stores

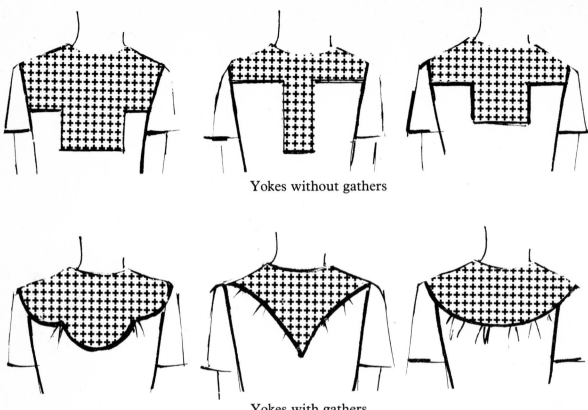

Yokes without gathers

Yokes with gathers

The yoke looks most effective when used with contrasting materials. With raglan and kimono sleeves the yoke may be symmetric or asymmetric. Yokes, with fullness or without, as illustrated.

The nearer the yoke line is to the point of the bust the less ease will result from the use of the entire basic dart, but the further the yoke line is from the bust point the more ease there will be.

Shoulder yoke : The shoulder yoke provides ease, keeping the shoulder line and neck line neat and smooth

Waist yoke : When waist yokes are introduced in a design the proportions of the yoke in relation to the rest of the design must be considered very carefully

Hip yoke : The purpose of the yoke at the hip is to provide a smooth, fitted hipline. This looks attractive when combined with pleats, gathers, or a circular skirt

This seam is often used for yokes and applied pieces. One section is lapped over the other and top stitched.

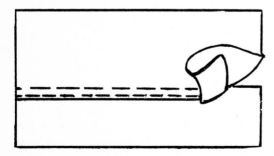

Adaptation of a suit

Design a selection of suits suitable for town wear. Take one of the designs, adapting the design six times by introducing a variation of Yokes in contrasting materials, collars and button placing.

Occasion : Town wear
Season : Spring
Fabric : Linen
Colour : Own choice. Contrasting
Market outlets : Medium price, Fashion store

DESIGN DETAILS

Make a collection of sketches in your sketch book of
design features, such as pockets, tabs, fastenings, belts,
seams and so on.
Design many variations as you compile your collection;
you will find this most useful when designing, as a
reference for ideas. Make notes of interesting details
you may see. These you will find in fashion
magazines, or by looking at displays in shop windows,
or attending fashion shows.
The sketch book is essential to every designer. All
students of design should begin to maintain one very
early in their career.

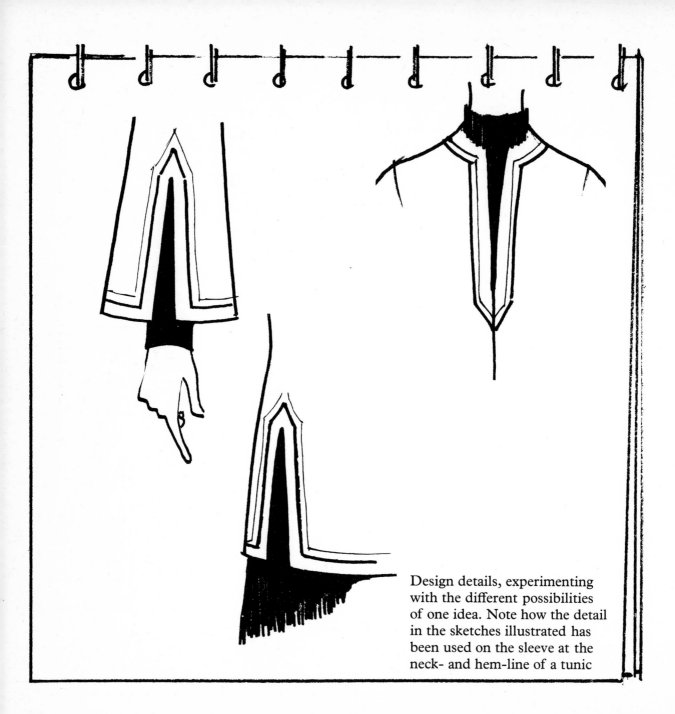

Design details, experimenting with the different possibilities of one idea. Note how the detail in the sketches illustrated has been used on the sleeve at the neck- and hem-line of a tunic

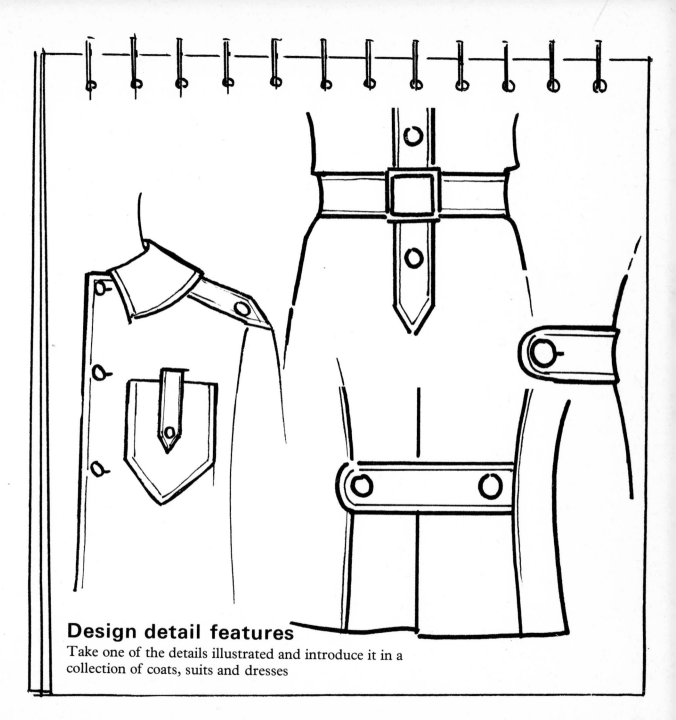

Design detail features

Take one of the details illustrated and introduce it in a
collection of coats, suits and dresses

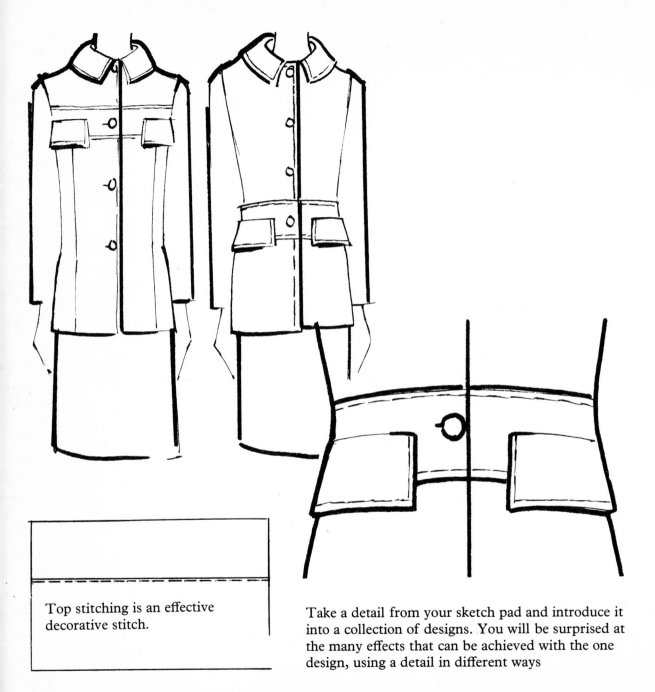

Top stitching is an effective decorative stitch.

Take a detail from your sketch pad and introduce it into a collection of designs. You will be surprised at the many effects that can be achieved with the one design, using a detail in different ways

Collars

The collar is a most important fashion feature on a garment. There is a variety of collar designs and shapes, but basically there are three main types:

1 Flat
2 Roll
3 Stand

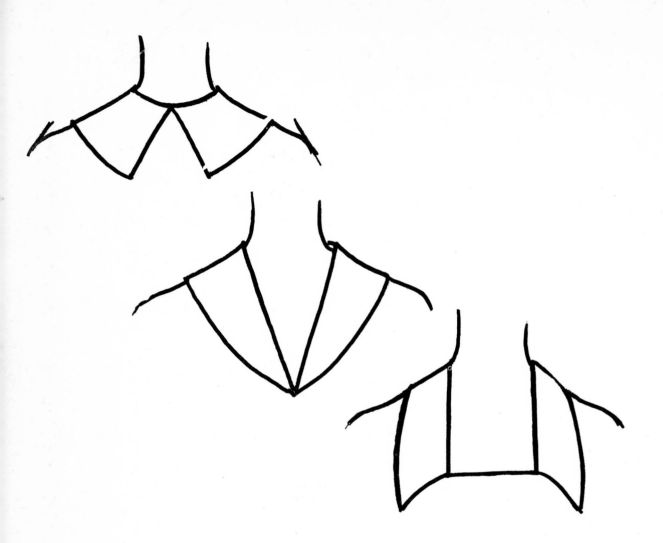

Flat collars

The flat collar may vary in width from an inch wide or as wide as the shoulders. You may design many variations from this collar. It is most helpful to make notes in your sketch book of any new ideas you may see.

A selection of flat collars

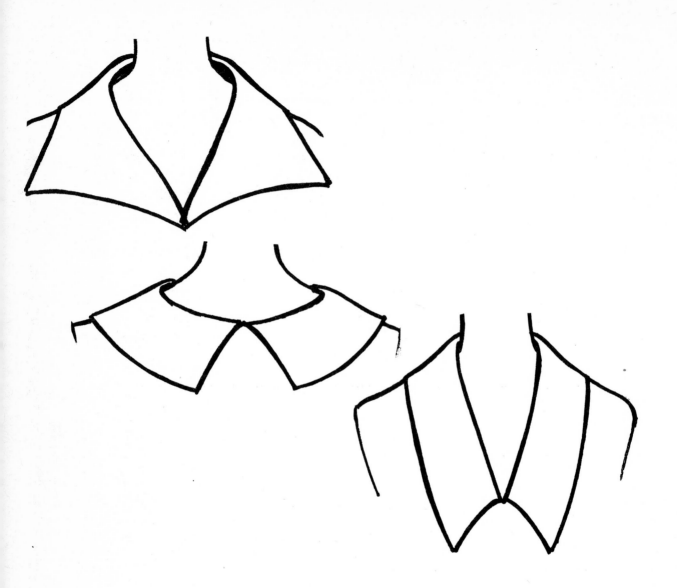

A selection of roll collars

The silhouette is created both by the depth of the roll
and by the shape of the free edge

A selection of roll collars

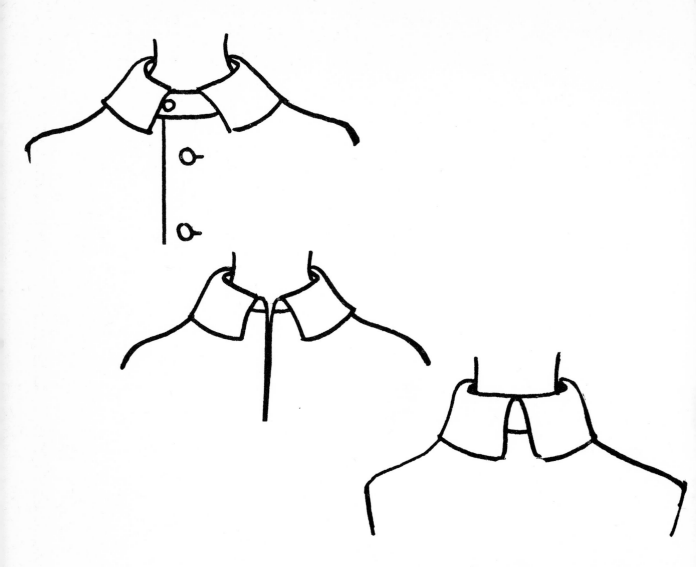

A selection of stand collars

Break line: The line where the roll leaves the stand is called the break line. The break is the point where a lapel starts to roll back from the front hem

The Stand: In rolled collars the part which provides the height of the collar is called the stand

A selection of stand collars

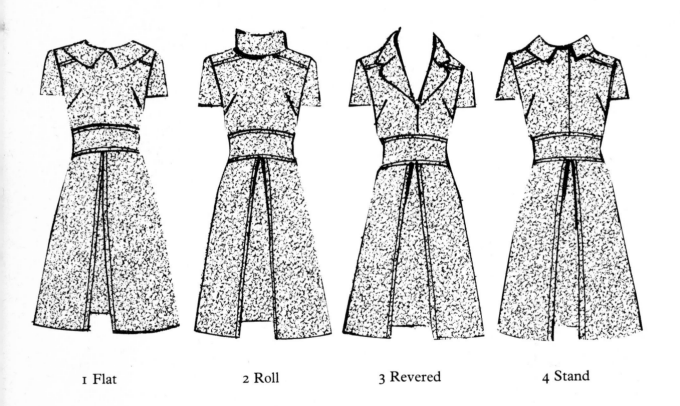

1 Flat   2 Roll   3 Revered   4 Stand

Collars

As an exercise, design a dress, a coat, or a suit. Then adapt your idea by introducing a different collar on the same design—as in the illustrations

Convertible Collar : This collar
is designed to be worn open or
closed

Tuxedo collar : A collar rolled
over and even in width,
extending to the front edge of
the garment

55

Roll collars : Any collar which rolls back and is not pressed flat

Peter Pan : This is a round flat collar and can be made as a one-piece or two-piece collar

Mandarin collar : Stand collar meeting at the front of the neck. As seen in the Mandarin dress

Cowl neckline : A soft, draped neckline. The bodice front is cut on the bias of the fabric to form soft folds

Boat neckline : A neckline following the curve of the collar bone

Halter neck : A neckline with a strap or built-up bodice in the front, fastening at the back of the neck

Shawl collar : A collar with a roll extending almost to the waist

Sailor collar : Square at the back, narrowing to a V at the front. As worn by sailors trimmed with braid

Sleeves

Sleeves may be divided into two basic types:
1 The set-in sleeve
2 The sleeve cut in one with the bodice
The shirt sleeve, Dolman sleeve, and Raglan sleeve
are variations of the set-in sleeve, but fit into a deeper
or an irregularly shaped armhole. The Kimono sleeve
is cut in one with the bodice. It can be made without
a gusset or with a two piece gusset.

Sleeve lengths

There are many variations of the sleeve length. When designing careful consideration should be given to the proportions of the sleeve in relation to the rest of the design

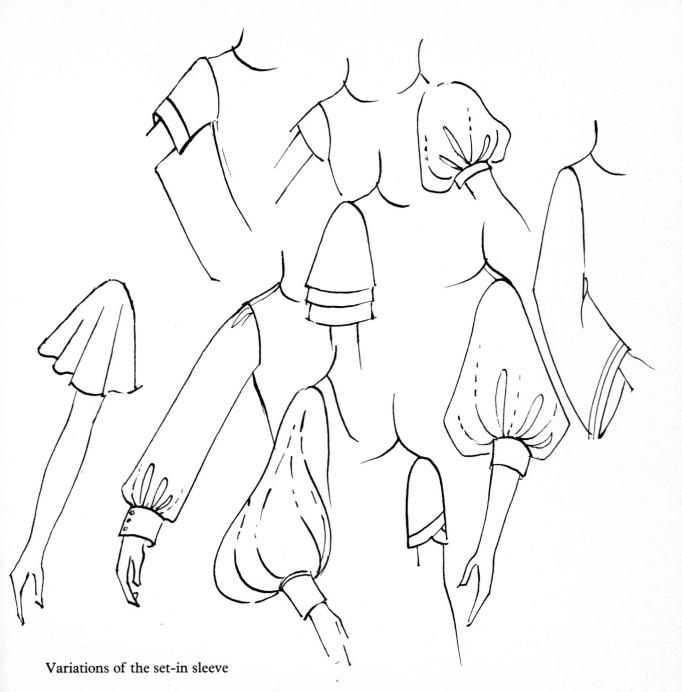

Variations of the set-in sleeve

Variations of the set-in sleeve

Sleeves cut in one with the bodice

1 Raglan
2 Saddle
3 Kimono
Design a selection of sleeves, and keep them for
further reference in your sketch book. When you see
an interesting design in a magazine, or on display,
make a note of it

A variation of armhole shapes

A variation of armhole shapes can result in a good
design. Note those illustrated and then design some
of your own. The suggested lines look most attractive
for evening wear and beach garments.

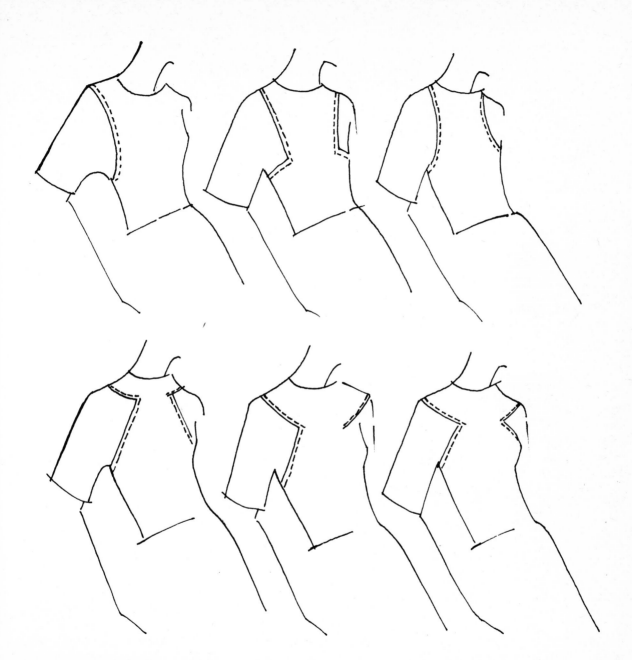

A variation of armhole shapes

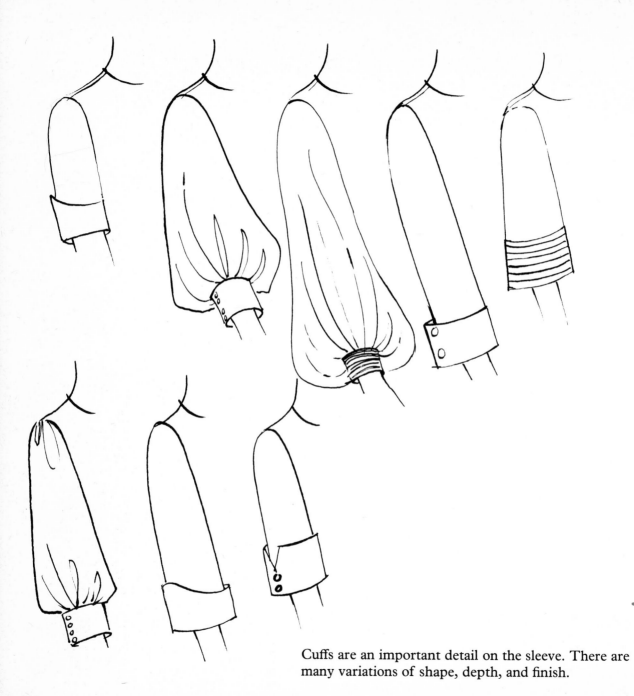

Cuffs are an important detail on the sleeve. There are many variations of shape, depth, and finish.

Pockets

Pockets are decorative and at the same time functional features. A number of adaptations can be designed from the three basic types illustrated.

The shape and size of the pocket in relation to the design must be considered with great care.

There are three types of pockets: The patch pocket, which is stitched on to the surface of the garment, the set-in pocket, for which a special opening is made in the garment, and the pocket set into a seam in the garment.

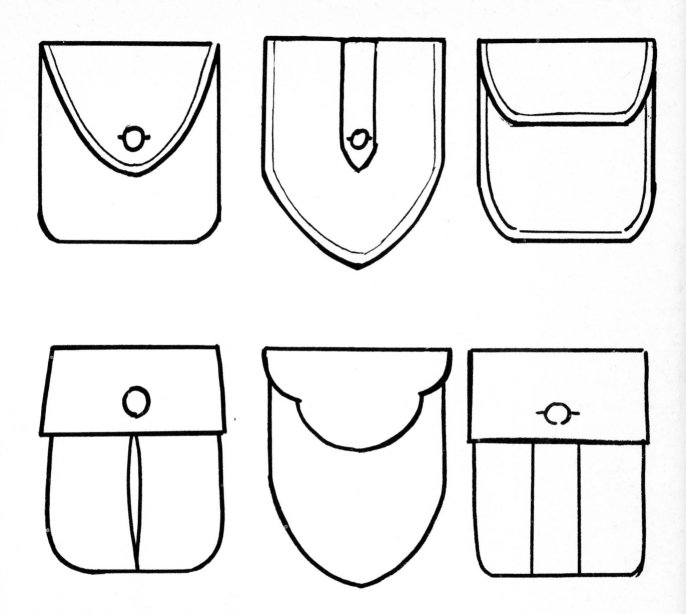

Patch Pockets: These are pockets which are applied
to the right side of the material. There are many
variations of shape. Illustrated here are only a few of
them. How many can you design?

Set-In Pockets: Set-in Pockets are obtained by cutting an opening in the garment.

There are three types of set-in pockets:

1 Welt
2 Bound
3 Flap

Welt pocket :

Jetted pocket :

Jetted pocket with flap.

Seam pockets : The placing of
pockets into a seam in the
garment.
(Note in the illustrations the
pockets have been indicated
with a thicker line.)

Fasteners

Fasteners may be decorative as well as being functional. An important feature on a garment, they have become a decorative fashion feature. Zip fasteners look decorative as well as being functional. They are effective when designing sports wear and industrial garments on front openings and pocket fastenings.

Lacing : Lacing drawn through eyelets. Thickness of lacing and eyelets vary according to the design

Snap fasteners : Snap fasteners may be obtained in many sizes. They may be used as a decorative feature as well as being functional. They look particularly good on sports wear and industrial garments.

Straps and buckles : Straps and buckles look effective when used with casual and sports wear. The straps can be made in self material or contrasting with buckles of metal, etc.

Buttons : Buttons may be used as a decorative feature
on a garment and they may serve a functional purpose.
When selecting buttons for a design take care in
considering the colour, texture and weight of the
material on which the buttons will be displayed. Also
consider with care whether you wish the button to be
the focal point of your design or to serve a functional
purpose only

Fly fastening : An attractive style of buttoning. It adds an interesting feature to a design. With this type of fastening the buttons are completely concealed

Rouleau fastenings : Roll or fold of fabric, used for piping and making loops for fastening.

Zip fasteners : Zip fasteners have become a feature in fashion design and are no longer simply a functional way of fastening. Many variations are now produced in different materials, weights of slides and colour.

Corded frogs : These may be
made from cording or braid

Loop button holes : Loops of
cord or self fabric serving as a
button hole

Drawstring : A drawstring or casing is a design feature which has many variations. It can be used decoratively with belts of various widths or ties.

Listed are some of the fastenings that have not been illustrated:
Chains
Hook and eye
Clips
Tie
Hardware fasteners
Buckles
Velcro
Belts of leather, metal, chains, etc.

Fly front fastening

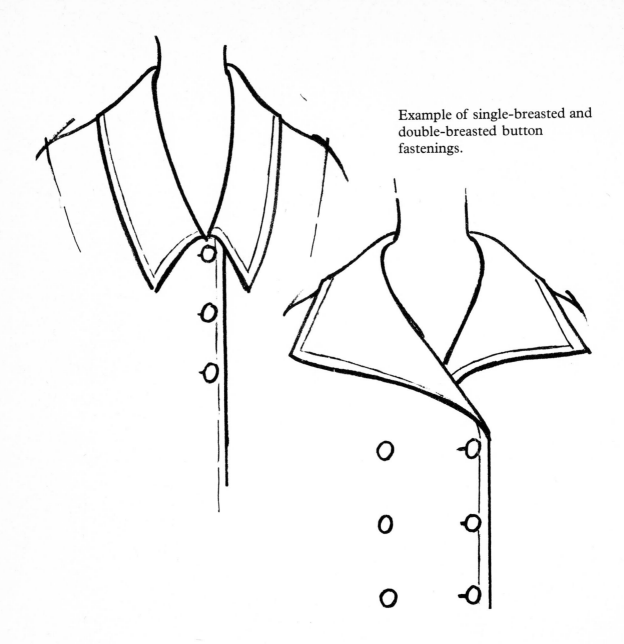

Example of single-breasted and
double-breasted button
fastenings.

As an exercise, design a collection of coats, using contrasting materials, (i.e. plain and textured), introducing a variation of sleeves and collars, and employing single and double-breasted fastenings, as illustrated.

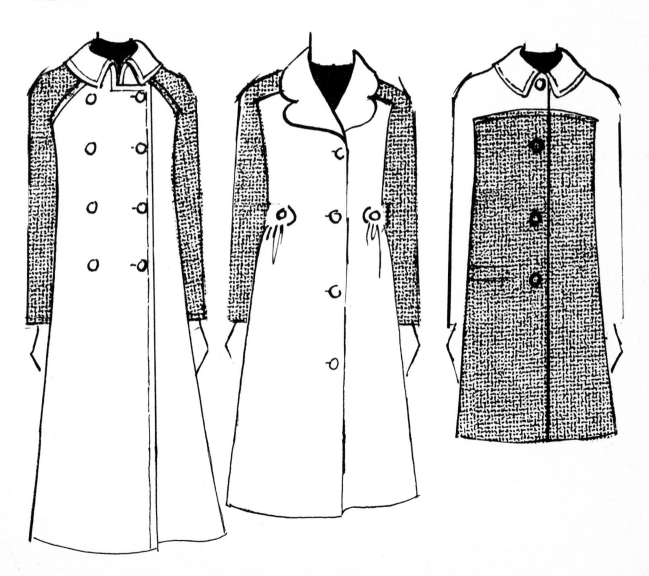

Uniform

Design a selection of overalls suitable for a supermarket assistant working in a food department. This uniform is to be worn by all the assistants. As the designer you must consider:

1 Working conditions—temperature, movement.

2 Age group. The age group will vary considerably, therefore the style must look attractive on all figure types and ages.

3 Colour and material. The image you project should be of cleanliness and neatness (the colour scheme should be contrasting).

4 The maintenance of materials. The uniforms would be cleaned frequently, therefore the material should be easy to maintain.

5 Fastenings—placing of pockets, cut and movement, should be considered carefully.

6 When asked to make a design of this kind the price of the garment would have to be considered and this of course would depend on how much the clients were prepared to spend.

TRIMMINGS

Many effects may be achieved with the use of trimmings. The following pages illustrate only a few of the large variety that are available and the way in which they are used.

List of trimmings

Cotton fringe
Wool fringe
Wool ruching
Nylon lace
Broderie anglaise trimming
Ostrich and maribou trimming
Plaited wool trimming
Sequin and beaded motif
Diamante trimming
Wool and cellophane trimming
Wool braid
Pleated nylon trimming
Nylon net ruching
Folded leather trimming
Plaited leather trimming
Rick-rack
Russian braid

Braids made in a variety of
materials may be obtained.
Many effects may be achieved.
Avoid using trimmings to
conceal bad workmanship.

Ready-made fringing

Braids and fringing

Fur trimmings : Design a selection of coats suitable for the Winter season. Introduce a variation of lengths, considering the proportions of the skirt length in relation to the bodice.

Occasion : Winter coat suitable for formal wear

Fabric : Wool tweed introducing fur trimming of fox

Market outlet : Model department in fashion store

*Note the use of beading on the
bodice cuffs and hem of stole*

Evening Wear

Design a selection of evening dresses and trouser outfits suitable for a young market, introducing beading as a feature.

Occasion : Evening wear suitable for—dinner party, theatre.

Season : Winter

Fabrics : Velvet, wild silk or chiffon.

Market Outlets : Young market, suitable for boutique

Ostrich feathers : Ostrich feathers make an attractive trimming on cocktail and evening dresses. Illustrated are a few examples of how ostrich feathers may be used. They can be obtained in a variety of colours and look most attractive when combined with materials such as chiffon, velvet, etc.

Often several feathers are carefully glued together as one. They are made from the wing or tail of the ostrich. They may be dyed in any colours and curled.

Fabric Treatments

Different effects may be achieved with all materials
by a variety of treatments. Listed and illustrated are
some of the more popular effects.

Bows
Ruffles
Ruching
Piping
Frills
Fringing
Scallops
Sheering
Machine embroidery
Pin tucks
Pleating
Rouleaus
Smocking
Quilting
Bias cut
Applique
Inset-pieces

Self fringing

Gather : To draw up a fabric by
one or more threads

Self fringe : The fringe made by
drawing threads of the fabric

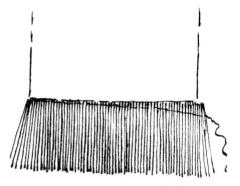

Ready made fringe : A heavy
fringe can be made from a fabric
and purchased ready-made

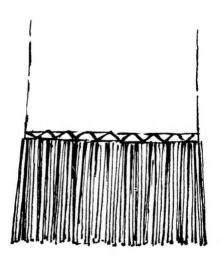

Scallops

Frills applied in a seam

Double Frills

Piping : Piping can be used set
in to a seam or as a surface
decoration. It is made by
covering cord with bias fabric

Unpressed, unstitched pleats or tucks create soft
folds. Decorative folds or drapery may be arranged in
horizontal, diagonal or curved lines. They may be
created by modelling the fabric on a dress form or
they can be created by the flat pattern method. The
designer will try out folds on different grains and
bias of the fabric

Tucks : A fold of fabric used as a
decorative feature, holding
fullness and used for shaping

Pin tucks : Tucks of a very
narrow width used on yokes,
sleeves, and cuffs, etc.

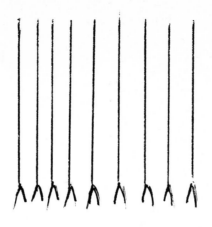

Graduated tucks : Tucks in a
series of width of which each
one is smaller than the one
below

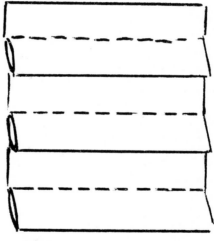

Tucks in groups : Tucks in
groups or spaced continuously
at waistline or sleeves and yokes,
etc

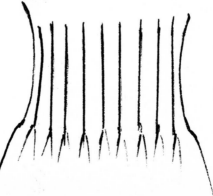

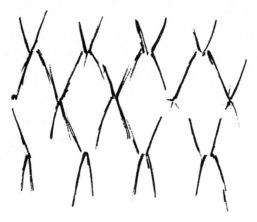

Smocking : Smocking is a decorative way of holding fullness in even folds. It looks most effective used on dresses, blouses, bodices, sleeves, etc

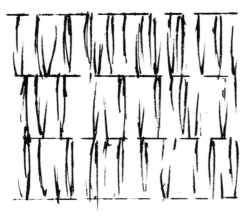

Shirring : Shirring is achieved by putting an elastic thread through the material. This creates the various effects which are illustrated

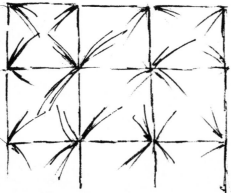

Quilting : Fine running stitches or machine stitches made through two thicknesses of material with light weight padding between

Shirring may be used on sleeves, waists, bodices, etc. with flattering effects.

Sunray pleats : Pleats from a central point radiating to the edge of the garment

Knife pleats : Similar to the accordion pleats, but must all face in the same direction

Accordion pleats : Very narrow straight pleats

Unpressed pleats : Soft pleats with edges rounded and left unpressed

Box pleats : Two flat folds with edges meeting inside

Inverted pleats : The reverse of the box pleat the edges meet on the outside of the garment

Evening separates

Design a selection of separates suitable for an evening
occasion at the theatre, dinner or dancing. Introduce
pleating as a feature in the designs (refer to fabric
treatments and pleating).

Occasion: Evening wear
Season: Summer
Fabric: Pure silk
Colour: Own choice of colour and Pattern
Market Outlet: Model department in fashion store

Shirring

Summer dresses

Design a selection of summer dresses suitable for a
young market. Introduce Shirring as a feature in the
designs.

Occasion: Late afternoon into evening
Season: Summer
Age group: Teenage
Suggested materials: Cotton Voile
Market Outlets: Fashion store, medium price

In-set pieces: Many effects may be obtained by inserting pieces of the material cut on the cross, or of contrasting colour and texture.

Appliqué: Appliqué is achieved by applying a design of a piece of fabric to another

Textures

Fabrics like line can also influence your design.
Texture and weight of the fabric are important as
they have a strong effect on the silhouette. There
may be great variety as between:
Rough and smooth textures
Stiff textures
Transparent textures
As a designer you should experiment, introducing
different textures together, trying out the many effects
that may be achieved.
It is a good idea to collect a variety of sample pieces
of fabrics which should be as varied as possible, i.e.
in contrasting colours, texture and weight. The sample
need only be a small size, 2 sq. inch. When designing
it is most useful to have a collection as a source of
inspiration. Experiment with contrasting materials
such as canvas, leather, wool, silk, p.v.c., fur, etc.

Contrasting materials and textures

Velvet bodice with chiffon skirt
and sleeves. Note the adaptation
of one design by introducing
bodice and sleeve variation

Contrast

With the use of contrasting fabrics many pleasing
effects may be achieved. On the following pages are a
number of design exercises showing the use of
contrasting fabrics in design. These are only a few of
the many effects you may obtain.

Set yourself some design exercises using contrasting
fabrics as a theme. First select some sample pieces;
the choice of the material is most important in that
the material should be suited to both the design and
the occasion for which the garment is designed.

Considerations when selecting contrasting materials
for the suitability of the design:

1 Contrast of colour and tones
2 Contrast of plain and patterned materials
3 Contrast textures, i.e.:

Leather and wool
Fur and velvet
Silk and tweed
Canvas and P.V.C.
Suede and Fur
Metal and Chiffon

1 Wool tweed and silk
2 Wool tweed and jersey

Note the use of fringing on the
stole and braid on the jacket.

Winter coats

Design a selection of coats to be made in contrasting fabrics of your own selection. Introduce variation of hemlines, considering the proportions of the design. Remember the many variations of pockets, collars, sleeves, seam placing, etc. that a designer can use.

Occasion : Town coat (formal wear)

Season : Winter

Fabrics : Own selection

Colour : Introduce the seasons current fashion colours

Market Outlet : Model department in fashion store

Contrasting fabrics in plain
wool combined with a patterned
fabric in wool.
Note the use of raglan and
kimona sleeve

Adaptation of a Design

The variation of one design adapted in different ways
may be achieved by working on one basic idea
Introducing:
1 Different materials
2 Contrast materials and textures
3 Variation of sleeves and collars
4 Style details of pockets
5 Seam placing
6 Belts and fastenings
7 Trimmings

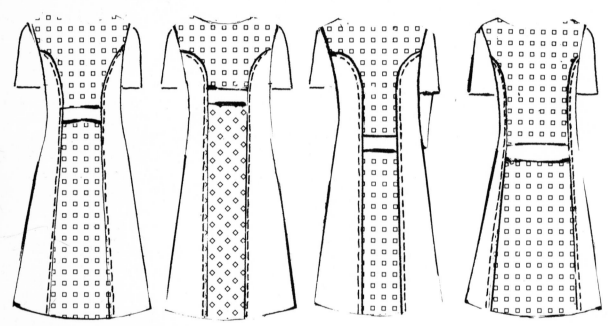

Adaptation of a day dress in
contrast materials. Note that
the simple adaptation has been
achieved by the placing of the
panel lines and half belt effect.

Note that some of the fitting
would be incorporated in the
panel lines

Note the use of waist yokes in
contrasting fabrics and the
variation of shapes

Variation of bodice shape and neck lines : Design a day
dress in contrasting material of your own choice,
introducing a variation of bodice shapes and neck lines

Adaptation of one basic dress
shape. This has been achieved
by placing the seam-lines on the
shoulders

Variations in seam placing (see how many you can develop by using this idea). Design some shapes of your own and introduce some different types of sleeves and collars as a variation on the theme

Note how one can adapt a
simple design with the use of
patterned and plain materials,
i.e. by introducing a band of
plain material in various ways

As an exercise design a basic dress shape. Use
patterned material with contrasting bands of plain
material of various widths and see how many effects
you can achieve

Design a selection of dresses in contrasting fabrics of your own choice, adapting your designs in different ways by introducing a variation of sleeves, yokes, and collars.

Occasion : Summer dresses suitable for summer holidays and travelling

Season : Summer

Fabrics : Cotton lawn.

Market Outlet : Medium price boutique for young market

PLAIN AND PRINT CONTRAST

Black and Black and white spot print

1 Blouse with *cowl* neckline and *bishop* sleeves with deep cuff and *boot button* fastening, worn with long skirt with slight flare and deep waist band.

2 Trouser outfit. Black, sleeveless top with *square neckline*, worn with black and white spot trousers, very flared.

3 Blouse with full *bell shape* sleeves, deep square neckline, worn with long skirt in black, with slight flare

Try sketching from the figures illustrated, then sketch some of your own. Should you find this difficult trace the figures from the book and sketch your designs on to them

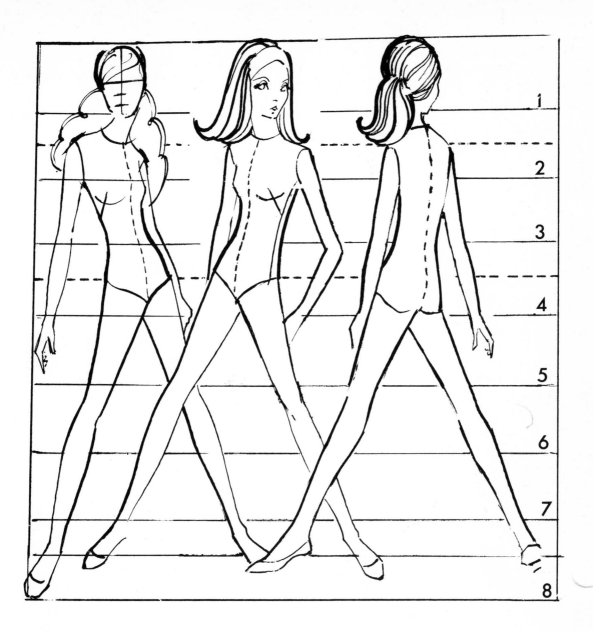

1

2

3

4

5

6

7

8

Back Views

Consider the back view of your designs. The main design interest may not always be on the front of the garment, it may be featured in the back in the form of draping, seaming, pleats, etc. When making a design feature at the back the designer would balance the front by keeping it simple.

SOME TECHNICAL DEFINITIONS

Block patterns : Basic pattern of a simplified design, frequently made of a strong paper. This is used for designing.

Boutique : Often a boutique is attached to a couture house. It consists of a small shop that sells accessories and separates and other individual garments. Boutiques can also be independent shops selling individual garments.

Fashion Buyer : A person who buys for a fashion department or fashion shop. He is usually also in charge of the department for which he or she buys.

Collections : The creations of a designer shown at fashion show. Generally Spring and Autumn are the two principle periods when the collections are shown to the press, buyers, and private clients. Some houses have a mid season fashion show.

Couturier : Male designer generally describing the owner of a dressmaking house.

Couturière : A woman dress designer.

Embroideries : This term means needlework the creations of designs on the material with cotton, metal, silk, wool or alternative threads. This needlework is produced by hand or machine. There are two main streams, i.e. Western and Eastern. The Western stream includes certain north african embroidery. The subdivisions are manifold. Listed are only a few of the many different types.
Berlin Work
Holbein
Hungarian Point
Irish Work
Japanese
Russia
Madras work

Jugoslavian work
Philippine
Turkish

Ergonomics : Ergonomics is a group of applied sciences which can assist the designer to produce designs that are functional and attractive for the suitability of the activity they have been designed for. It can be that the main Ergonomic consideration is the maintenance and the ease and range of movement.

Fashion illustrator : The fashion illustrator works for magazines, newspapers, trade journals etc., usually known for their own style of drawing. The work involves attending fashion shows, the sketching of the garments shown, also illustrating fashions for stores magazines, and posters etc.

Fashion journalist : The fashion journalist reports on fashion. Attending fashion shows and fashionable events writing articals for magazines, newspapers, trade journals, etc. Some journalists do illustrate their own articals, others work in conjunction with the

fashion illustrator. Fashion journalists have their own style of writing as a fashion illustrator has when sketching.

Fittings : To rectify the shape of a garment to fit the wearer by adjusting the details.

Godet : A triangular piece of fabric let into the skirt to give a flared effect. It may be inserted into a seam or a slit from the hem to any point depending on the design.

Hanger Appeal : A design with hanger appeal is one that has been designed to be displayed in a show room on a hanger to attract the client. Many attractive designs will not display well on hangers, but when designing for a particular market such as chain stores or department stores, this appeal is an important consideration, when garments are displayed on rails.

Haute Couture : Couture (from the french) meaning sewing or dressmaking. It is a collective term to describe dressmaking houses.

Fashion model : The model displays the creations for sale in Couture houses. Also models working free-lance, working through agencies for Couture houses, wholesale firms, stores, and advertising, magazines etc.

Mass production : Production of garments in quantities, mainly made by machinery. Mass production is for large wholesale markets.

Pattern cutter : The pattern cutter cuts an accurate pattern from the designers original.

Pattern grader : The grader will grade the patterns to different sizes for production.

Peplum : The peplum is a separate flared piece of fabric extending from the waist to the hip line.

Retail : Retail is selling of garments to the consumer

through stores, shops, boutiques etc.

Sample machinist : The sample machinist makes the sample garments under the direction of the designer, experimenting with different collars, sleeves, seams etc.

Synthetics (man-made fibres): Fabrics made through chemical processes. They were first used as substitutes for natural materials. The term applies to-day for describing man-made fibres. (Nylon, Terylene, Cotton Polyester, Tricel/Rayon etc.).

Textile firms : Textile firms specialise just as fashion firms do. Some specialise in Silk, wool, and others in Knits or novelty fabrics. Their ranges and prices vary

Toile : A French term standing for cloth mostly of cotton or linen fabric. A muslin copy of a design, this is often bought by firms who only wish to copy the original model and adapt the design for their own market.

Wholesale : Wholesale is selling of garments usually in large quantities to the retailers. Wholesalers have usually showrooms where they display the garments to the buyers.